PETALS OF THE ROSE

SUE VINCENT

INDEX

*"I wished a companion to lie near me in the starlight,
silent and not moving, but ever within touch.
For there is a fellowship more quiet even than solitude,
and which, rightly understood, is solitude made perfect."*

Robert Louis Stevenson

INTRODUCTION

Be welcome in this moment and in this place.

The meditations in this book are guided journeys, all of which have been used during workshops run by the Silent Eye, a not-for-profit teaching school of modern mysticism. The meditations are designed to allow you to explore the levels of your being.

On one level, they are just stories within which you should immerse yourself in imagination. Though no story is ever 'just' a story... On other levels of consciousness, they may act as keys to unlock hidden corners of mind and being.

The book begins with very simple visualisations, for those with no experience at all of this type of active meditation in which we choose to follow a pre-defined path.

Walk each journey within your imagination, as if you were living it, rather than being just an observer.

Feel yourself within the story as it unfolds on the

canvas of mind.

Feel the sensations, use your senses to experience the full range of the story, from touch to taste, smell to sound. Allow each meditation to become immersive.

Some people find that it can be useful to record the meditations and listen to them rather than reading them.

It is also essential to remember that what arises from these inner landscapes will be purely personal and will be best interpreted by asking questions of *yourself.*

To begin, find a time and place where you will not be disturbed. Mute the telephone, close the door. You may light a candle or burn a fragrance if you wish, these things can help define a moment out of time.

Now, sit comfortably, with your body well supported.

Relax and breathe deeply in whatever rhythm feels most natural to you.

Close your eyes and when you are ready, you may begin...

SEEKING FOR THE SELF *(Simple Visualisation)*

Close your eyes, relax your body, breathing easily and deeply. Relax your shoulders, let the tension seep away from your neck... allow your muscles to relax.

You are standing in a green place, a place of life and death where the seasons turn. There is grass beneath your feet, trees rustle in the breeze. Feel how your body is poised and balanced, notice the small movements of your toes and the soles of your bare feet upon the earth...the muscles of your legs tightening and relaxing second by second to hold you steady. *Feel* that constant adjustment of balance as your body responds to each minute shift...

Explore the sensations in your body right now... at *this* moment... feel the tensions and small aches... the tickle... the odd itch on your skin...

Notice your eyelids flickering and your eyes moving beneath them.

Be aware of the shifting colours of light that penetrate your eyelids.

You cannot yet see... there is no detail... but your mind holds a picture of this place

C it up in your imagination. Look at the scene... the colours, the shapes... things your memory understands...

Feel the touch of the air on your cheeks, notice its movement... follow it within your body as you breathe it in... feel its movement in your nose and your throat... notice how your lungs expand and contract, filling and emptying to a steady rhythm.

The smell of autumn is in the air; a rich, damp smell. You can taste it with each breath and it calls up memories of other autumns, of kicking piles of fallen leaves, plucking apples from the tree, collecting conkers... the smell of childhood and bonfires...

How does that make you feel? Are you happy? Sad? Bored?. Curious?

Notice your emotions... are they here and now? Are they called up by memory?

What are emotions? Where do they belong?

Are they part of your body?

Do they come from the same awareness that notices them?

The same as memory?

Now... notice that you *are* noticing.

Be aware of your awareness observing your body, your emotions, your memories...

Where is it, that awareness?

Is that awareness part of your body? Is it a physical thing? Ask the question.

Follow it within. How many levels of your self can you see? Your body, sensations, memories, emotions, so many thoughts flitting through your mind....

Which one is 'you'? Any of them? All of them?

YOU are watching all of them...

But... who and where are YOU?

Sit with that thought for a while, let it roll around your mind... but do not stress over finding an answer.

Then, When you are ready, open your eyes. Move your limbs, look around the room to ground yourself and bring you back to normality.

The meditation is over.

THE DRAGON'S EGG

Close your eyes, relax your body, breathing easily and deeply. Relax your shoulders, let the tension seep away from your neck. Allow your muscles to relax.

Around you is the world you know... the path beneath your feet, the trees, the sky. Feel yourself there.

Before you is a strange structure. It looks like an egg, but man sized, far bigger than you...

Its surface is like glass, reflecting distorted images of the world around you. Colours shift across its curves as light plays within a jewel. In its side, you can see the trace of what looks like a door. There is no handle. but as you look at it, seeing it for the first time, the outline becomes clearer, as if your own awareness makes it visible. You place your hand upon it and the side of the egg dissolves.

You go through the doorway into the space within...

Around you is the world you know. The path beneath your feet, the trees, the sky...feel yourself there...

look around. It is the same, yet you seem to see it differently. Everything has clean lines, the colours are brighter, the air warmer and the light clearer.

Before you is another egg, even larger than the last. Its surface glistens with colour and light. You look for a door and as you do it becomes visible, responding to your quest.

Again you step through. Around you is the world you know... the path beneath your feet, the trees, the sky... yet the light is so bright that you can almost see through everything, as if it is made of glass, or many coloured jewels capturing the light.

This time the egg is huge. Somewhere in the back of your mind you wonder how all this could be contained within the first. Its surface glows with jewel coloured rainbows, as water held by some arcane force, flowing within itself. It is not reflecting the light, it IS light, held in this form... holding itself.

Again a door appears as you look for it... you walk through. Around you is a world you know; it feels like home, familiar...secure... yet it is not the world you know. There is nothing within except a light which flows around you, swirling rainbows dancing in joy...

You reach out a hand and colours cluster around it like butterflies. Within the dancing light is the world you know... shapes and forms coming into being and dissipating ... the forms of life...even the very air that you breath is alive with colour.

And before you is an egg... vast as a mountain. Your awareness is the key that makes visible the door. You walk towards it and enter in... and beyond the door is only Light... and within that Light, is all you have ever known and all you will ever be.

Bathe in that Light

You are content. At peace. Draw all your spirit needs from that inexhaustible stream of Light. Rest a while in on its peace.

When you are ready, open your eyes. Move your limbs, look around the room.

The meditation is over.

CRYSTAL MIRRORS

Close your eyes, relax your body, breathing easily and deeply. Relax your shoulders, let the tension seep away from your neck. Allow your muscles to relax.

You sink deep into the soft, supporting warmth of the chair. You hold a crystal, a perfect sphere , flawless. You cradle it in your hand, feeling its weight. It is not cold, but warm, borrowing life from your skin. You can feel a gentle pulsing in its surface, as if it is alive. You wonder if this, too, is just borrowed from your body, measuring the beating of your own heart..

The light plays over its surface. Distorted reflections come and go, flexing in time with your slow, deep breath. Your eyes lose focus, sinking into the depths of the crystal and vision blurs.

You feel a shifting motion, not unpleasant, as if you are floating gently through space. Your focus returns, sharper than ever before. Everything around you has an unusual clarity. You cannot tell whether the crystal has expanded or if you have become very small, but you are within the crystal sphere.

Looking down at your feet, you can see below you the misty outline of a hand holding the sphere safely, cupped around it.

Around and above you, the inner structure of the crystal is visible. Planes and angles catch the glow, throwing rainbows of soft colour in every direction. It is a place of light and beauty. Every facet of the crystalline structure acts as a mirror, reflecting your image back at you from every angle.

It is like being inside a hall of mirrors.

You have a fleeting memory of fairgrounds and childhood as you remember the distorted shapes echoing your movements. Yet here there is no distortion. Just perfect clarity.

For a moment you are surprised. You do not seek out your own reflection as a rule, but here you are surrounded by images of yourself. There is nowhere to hide in this place. Everywhere you look your own image is reflected back. You are alone with yourself.

Yet you are perfectly calm.

There is no emotion except curiosity. You are observing, detached... standing apart from yourself. There is nothing to hurt or harm, nothing to distress you, nothing but observation and a desire to know and understand this stranger.

You have never seen yourself reflected quite like this before. The crystal plane between you and your image acts as both a lens and a shield.

You reach out to touch the crystalline surface in front of you. The reflection reaches out to you and your hands meet on the crystal mirror. Yet this is not a cold, impersonal touch, there is life in it. Warmth.

Your own eyes gaze out at you as if you are standing beyond the crystal. You see many reflections of yourself. From every angle, all at once. All perfectly clear.

Take your time. There is no hurry. Look at this reflection as if it were a stranger you are meeting for the very first time. It is just a reflection... it cannot see you, cannot feel you, cannot think. Without you to give it life, it does not exist.

Look at your image in the mirror. Look at yourself.

Look at your clothes, your shoes, your hair... really *look* at the choice of colours, the shapes and styles.

This stranger in the mirror... what do these things say to you about that person? What image are they projecting into the world?

What do they want the world to believe about them?

Notice the way your image stands. How the feet... your feet... are planted on the ground, how you hold your spine. Look at your shoulders, is there tension there?

Tiredness?

Has life and experience marked them... or are they relaxed and free as you move?

Who is this person in the mirror? What would you feel about them if you met them for the first time?

Now look at your hands as they are reflected.

How are you holding them?

What are you doing with them?

Are they comfortable... or do they seem nervous? Are they strong and confident... are they practical... expressive?

What do you notice about them? What thoughts drift through your mind?

Hold out your hand to your reflection again. Do you want to take the hand of the person in the mirror? Why? What do you feel about them?

Now look at the face... the jaw... the mouth...

Read the story of the person written there.

Are you smiling? Is the mouth worried...bitter ... kind.... Sad... gentle?

Are there lines around the eyes? What caused them... laughter... tears... both?

Are there lines on the brow? What do they tell you? Were they written by concentrating... working too hard... worrying too much... or laughter?

If this face smiled at you in the street, would you smile back?

Now look into the eyes... deep into those eyes... Look as if you would ask the most important question in the world...

Who is looking back at you? Who is this person?

What drives them? What emotion is written on that face, in those eyes?

What type of person do *you* think they are...

If you met this stranger, what would attract you to them?

Look deeper... beyond the surface. Look through the eyes to the mind... the thoughts... the person...

The crystal rainbows swirl and dance, leading you inwards, into the reflection. You follow them... still curious...

What do you see behind those eyes that draws you deep into the mind of this person?

Rainbow light dances through the thoughts, hopes and fears, lighting them p, one by one, letting you see into all the private places... all the hidden corners... melting the cobwebs and opening the doors of dreams...

Follow the rainbow colours as they dance... what do you see there?

Now, look deeper.

Deeper still.

Look into the heart; the rainbows light your way, playing softly in the dark corners, casting out shadows ... dancing...

What is there in that heart? What do you read there... What do you see....

Who *is* this person...?

Now, follow the rainbow light as it comes back to the surface of the mirror. Look again at the image you see.

Would you count this person amongst your friends?

Would you trust them with your innermost thoughts?

Would you trust them with your life?

The dancing rainbows cloud the mirror, covering its surface. All the other reflections seem to shift and move, melding into one. As you watch, you see all the fragments meld into a single image...you, yourself... and the rainbows dance in beauty around it.

Your reflection smiles and holds out its hands to you...

As it does so, you feel the same smile upon your own face... in your own eyes... and your hands follow its movements... you too are but a reflection.

As your hands touch you become one with your image, melting together, a perfect match...

Your vision loses focus, the rainbows cloud your sight and you lose yourself in their beauty.

The soft light caresses your skin, your mind and your heart... you feel warm and at peace, content.

Through the swirling colours you glimpse something else. A pair of eyes... a shape, a form...

And you know that you are its reflection... and it is looking at you... through the crystal...

You move towards it and it approaches you, mirroring your movements, holding out its arms...

As you enter that embrace, your vision fades, leaving only a sense of warmth and beauty.

Peace.

Wholeness...

Stay with that feeling for a while.

Then, when you are ready, feel the chair beneath you, warm and comfortable... feel the floor beneath your feet as you return, relaxed, at peace.

Move your feet, your hands...

There is no hurry

When you are ready, open your eyes. Move your limbs, look around the room.

The meditation is over.

BEYOND THE FALL

Close your eyes, relax your body, breathing easily and deeply. Relax your shoulders, let the tension seep away from your neck... allow your muscles to relax.

Feel the earth beneath your feet... feel the life of earth around you.

You are walking through a green wood; it feels like spring. You sense the small creatures in the undergrowth, bustling busily, focussed on their needs. Birds sing in the trees... the world is alive with promise; faint perfumes rise from flowers that star the grass. It is beautiful and peaceful here, like the first morning of the world...

You walk deeper into the wood. The trees are filled with fruit, it is a joyous place of plenty/ Shafts of sunlight, warm and golden pierce the canopy of leaves, insects hum in the heat. It is hot.

You hear a sound... the rushing of a stream and follow it. Louder and louder it roars. You come out of the trees onto a clearing, perfectly round... at its centre a pool of water crystal clear, above a sky of deepest blue, noon and midnight, scattered with stars that echo the white flowers starring the grass, yet at the zenith the sun shines clear, mirrored in the pool.

Around the pool is a circle of stones, tall and ancient, scarred and worn. Lichen grows an intricate lace on their surface, all the colours of earth are there.

You rest for a while, picking the tiny flowers, nine of them. Like a child you make a daisy chain of them and hang it around your neck.

At the centre of the pool a waterfall pours down the face of a sheer cliff. As you watch the waters part in their falling you catch a glimpse of a cave and within a white fire burning...

Stripping off your garments you wade into the pool the crystal waters are cold on your skin. Your reflection follows you, your steps are hampered by the water through which you wade, the resistance makes the crossing difficult but you persevere, drawn by the cave behind the Fall the chill of the pool makes you long for the half glimpsed flames.

Water crashes around you as you reach the fall...should you continue? You could go back and warm yourself in the sunlight?

You go on, pushing through the cascade until your feet touch dry rock beneath...

There is a passageway beyond the fall, and deep within the earth the glimmer of flames...

Shivering you walk on, naked in the darkness...Behind you the noise of the world recedes... ahead the flame beckons; you walk on into silent stillness...

Beyond the flame stands a figure, hooded and robed in shadow. You cannot see its face, there is a strangeness about it. Your senses do not penetrate the shadows, yet it is almost familiar... there is a sense of recognition, of finding something lost, something long hidden or discarded, rejected .forgotten emotions stir,

You cannot say if the figure is that of a man or a woman, old or young...

Still as a statue it stands as you approach the only movement the dance of shadows cast by the flames it exudes such life and strength that you know it is not stone.

The cave is warm, womblike, dark...except for the flame... a fire which rises without fuel from the centre of the cave.

You are afraid... or are you? You feel that you should be afraid... yet   you are not...awed, perhaps....

moved by the power in this figure and in the white heat of the flame. You left fear behind with your garment, no more than a habit ... an expectation.

Here you are naked; all fear is gone, all expectation dissolved.

You hold out your arms to the flame seeking warmth; the figure mirrors your movement, it seems as if it reaches out to you.

Your fingers touch through the flame, your nakedness illuminated by the white fire, the figure deep in shadow.

You feel drawn and stand within the white flame....the figure stepping forward to meet you.

You are so close, as close as dancers, as mother and child, =as lovers...

A feeling of deep love floods through you.

Moved by some impulse you take the chain of flowers from around your neck and place it on the hooded head like a crown. The shadowy figure mirrors your every move and in turn crowns you with a circlet of white fire... lovers exchanging rings, a marriage deeper than blood, Sovereigns crowning their consort, eternally bound.

In that moment you understand... you are filled with love for this shadow self... and embrace the shadowy form, taking it into your arms as it takes you into its own.

You are filled with a strange alchemy of completeness.

You look within yourself and see the shadow and the light... the shadow that is the darkness against which the light is seen...

...and the fire leaps around the two that have become one.

When you are ready, open your eyes. Move your limbs, look around the room.

The meditation is over.

MEMORY BOX

Close your eyes, relax your body, breathing easily and deeply. Relax your shoulders, let the tension seep away from your neck... allow your muscles to relax.

You are climbing a dark staircase. It spirals round and round, lightless. You feel your way, a little uncertainly in the dark. Round and round, guiding our steps with your hands on the rails. You know the way... you have always known but you seldom come here....not often.

Your feet stop before a door. You feel the rough surface in the dark, old wood beneath your fingertips.

From around your neck you take a chain. Feeling carefully in the blackness you select the larger of two keys and fumble to find the lock. You insert the key and turn it, then open and step through the door.

You find yourself in a dark space. It is quiet and still, and seems far from your everyday life.

For a moment just enjoy the warm darkness.

There is a slight smell of wood and dust.

It is a homely place. Familiar somehow.

A light flickers, then gradually warms to a pale light, growing in strength.

You are in an attic.

Around you are piled boxes and packages. Some you recognise, others are mysterious shapes in the shadows.

There is a rocking horse, battered and dusty... old clothes peek out of cobwebbed bags... you remember them... a dress your mother once wore, your favourite jumper when you were little. Bags of toys, a teddy bear... musical instruments and old records. There are piles of books and papers...children's stories, adventures... school text books.

Looking round, you remember them all.

They take you back...

Things catch your eye, taking you backwards, backwards in memory...

Snatches of melody... You remember that song, can hear it playing on the radio... you remember, fleetingly, where you were... who you were with. You remember how it made you feel.

You recall that outfit... it was a special outfit. for a special day...

Memories return...

You see the items dance across the screen of memory like an old film. You watch faces, some almost forgotten... hear voices and words... odd moments of memory spring to life.

All around you are things that remind you of happy times....

You are safe here in this place, surrounded by the whispers of laughter... friendship... joy.... And love.

You wander around the attic, exploring memories that make you smile. You have stored these things here, kept them forever, because they are special and precious to you.

You take your time, for here there is no time. Just memories to explore, bathing in the joy of recall. All the little things, all the gifts life has given you. Feel them again. Feel them part of you always.

You smile with tenderness and memory.

All of this is here... now... still... forever part of who you are...

And yet, there is something odd about the place... something missing... something strangely flat... as if everything is lacking a dimension.

In the centre of the attic is a space...

In the centre of the space, away from the clustered treasures... there is a heavy chest.

It is iron bound, made of ancient wood.

Traces of paint shadow its surface.

You brush the dust away. On the lid is your name, written by the hand of a child. Your handwriting.

Beneath the name are three words....

Danger... keep out...

There are chains around the box, heavy chains. You touch them and they are cold on your skin. They are held together with padlocks... big, heavy, serious padlocks... Three of them. The chest is secure...

You remember the second key on the chain around your neck, resting cool against your skin.

You are afraid... you know the chest is yours... it has your name on it...

You have the key....

You do not recognise the chest...

Yet you wrote your name on it long ago.

Slowly, carefully, you kneel in the dust. You take the key and open the padlocks, one....two... three...

You let the chains slide to the floor....clinking together as they fall....

You lift the lid.... Slowly, the hinges creak with disuse, until you stare into the chest....

Inside there are packages, tightly wrapped and tied with string; all very neat and secure.

They are wrapped in paper of different colours... black and grey, dull, dark red and dingy brown....

It feels like a Christmas nightmare with a pile of gifts you are afraid to unwrap.

You do not know what the parcels may hold.

You take the package on the top of the pile. You feel it as you did as a child, trying to guess what it contains. It almost feels alive in your hands, unpleasant. But nothing could be alive in that chest... it has been locked for a lifetime.

The pale string unties easily...

The dingy paper unwraps ...

You stare at what you have found...

Another memory...

Another image of a time long past...

But this one is not joyful... it hurts....

Or it did.. once upon a time...Here it no longer hurts...

You can see it, remember it, understand it.

You can know it, but it cannot hurt you... not in this place.

You take the object in your hands, feeling its surface. It was a bad time... very emotional, horribly painful.

That was then... But *this* is now....

You look up and another memory catches your eye. Of course it would... that was a much happier moment, but it goes *with* the object in your hands. The two are part of the same time, part of the same story. It makes you smile as you see how the two are linked

You get up and take the object from the chest to the happy memory and place the two together. You can see how they fit together, almost like pieces of a puzzle. The hurt only mattered because of the joy. The pain was only there because you could feel the happiness that was its frame. But together they tell a story that is you.

You decide to leave them together; the dark memory does not need to be hidden... not any more. The thought makes you smile.

You return to the box, unwrapping another parcel. This time it holds fear. You remember it, you can taste it, you do not want to look at it... the choice is yours to make.

But you can.. and you do...

Again you recognise the happy object in the room that comes from the same time, the same story.

Again you take the dark memory to the bright and see how the two are only whole when they are together.

You go back to the chest...

One by one, you take the objects out.

You look back at all you have kept here, under lock and key, chained away from sight.

You remember why you hid them here, hiding them from yourself, not wanting to look... afraid to look... seeing your fears again, your mistakes, the things that made you weep, the things that made you squirm or feel ashamed... the things that hurt the child inside.

You take each object to the happier memory in full view in the room, the one from the same time, place, person. You see how they fit together and how necessary it is that they be together.

And as you look at the dark and bright together, you see that it is the shadows that make the colours seem brighter and throw them into relief, adding to their beauty.

You know why you hid them. You were afraid... a child afraid of the darkness in your own life... afraid of the darkness in yourself....

But the attic is now a place of warmth and light and colour.

You feel at ease.. at peace... happy...

Around you are the memories of your life but they are not just soulless objects they are fragments of your story.

Small reminders of who you were, are, may yet be.

Your life, your emotions, thoughts, actions, relationships, fragments of who you are. You look around with acceptance, compassion and love.

There is one more package... one last... a tiny parcel you almost missed. It is wrapped in what looks like an old sweet paper... bright and shiny...

You reach down into the depths of the chest and lift it out. It feels light and warm. You want to laugh for sheer joy. You unwrap the parcel...

As you move the paper aside something streams from the tiny package in your hand.

It is alive.

Golden, like sunlight.

Silver, like stardust.

Gentle as summer rain.

It wraps around you, settling over in the attic and everything looks fresh and new, sparkling and clean.

In wonder, you take a deep breath, drawing in the golden, glorious light...

Breathing in joy...

Understanding...

Breathing in Love...

At the door you take a last look at the room.. so full now of colour and life. You close the door behind you with a smile.

You will be back.

When you are ready, open your eyes. Move your limbs, look around the room.

The meditation is over.

CONSUME THE WORLD

Close your eyes and prepare for a guided journey.

Relax, breathe deeply, gently, silently…

There is only silence… nothing else… silence and utter darkness around you. You breathe and you cannot hear your breath… yet you can feel the life within you… feel your heart beating, a steady rhythm in your chest.

The silence seems to deepen, weaving itself around you like a shroud, you can almost hear it beating but nothing can breach this perfect stillness and it seems to you as if the silence too is alive that it too has a heartbeat if only you could hear it….

The absence of light and sound leave you feeling lost… you do not know where you are… or what you are… who you are… you cannot see… you dare not move… you can hear nothing…

In the darkness you raise your hands before you, straining to see them… to see something… anything… in the black velvet that surrounds you.

The dearest wish of your heart is to see...

And then, there is a light... a tiny, flickering flame... so small you would not see it were there any other light.

It dances before you. Your eyes are fixed on this point of light... you see the flame, blue and gold, but you do not know, cannot tell, how far away it may be. It is so small...

You hold out your hand and to your surprise, the tiny flame alights there... It is *very* small... barely a spark... yet it is perfect and dances on the palm of your hand, casting a small glow about it, illuminating your fingers with a pale light.

It is all you can see... and in this blackness... all your attention is focused on the flame. You have nothing else... know nothing else. Only this.

Your attention is fixed on the flame. You watch the movements of the dance... almost, almost you can feel a pattern, a rhythm here too. You watch the colours shifting... green... blue... yellow... gold...random flashes of life in the palm of your hand. It is beautiful... delicate... fearless...

You feel yourself drawn to it... and the stronger that feeling grows the more you are convinced that the flame, too is growing... or perhaps you are shrinking... you cannot tell... there is only you and the flame...nothing to compare to... nothing to judge by...

And it does not matter.

The flame that rested in the palm of your hand has grown... it fills your hand...the only real thing in your world.... A gift in the darkness. You watch the colours shift and play. There is no heat... just a pleasant warmth... the caress of a summer breeze upon your skin.

There is joy in the dance of the flame... you hold up your other hand and the flame spills over into your cupped hands... You watch it grow... Now you begin to hear a whispered sound... the song of the flame, almost beyond hearing...

Now you hold it in your arms it like a babe, cradling it like a babe and you feel something stir within you, as if you held a newborn child, fragile and precious. And still it grows... and the sound is a little louder... like a whisper... a small voice that calls to you in the silence... and you yearn to hear... to understand. To see. And to know...

Soon, the flame has grown so wide, so deep, so beautiful, that your arms open wide to embrace it, holding it to you, feeling the light bathe you. And in its light you can see your arms, your legs, your body, you can see yourself...

Now the flame is as tall as you, taller, deeper, brighter, and as you reached out to hold it, now it, in turn, embraces you, engulfing you... bathing you in light.

The flame is so bright, so beautiful, flashing colours all around you, that you can no longer see yourself... and you no longer care….

The flame bathes you in its light… and fear falls away… you are clean, baptised in fire… fresh and new as the phoenix…reborn. You are nothing and everything, you are yourself and you are fire, you are nothing and you are light…

Your senses reach out from the flame into the darkness … you can feel the world there… feel the sadness and the joy…. The hope and the tears…. The pain and poverty, beauty and laughter. But you… you are flame… and this is the fuel that feeds you… you open yourself to the world and draw it in, feeding from it… consuming it.

Yet the more you draw into your flame, the brighter you burn, the clearer the world becomes, sharper, more detailed… more visible… until you can see every detail, understanding the pattern of days. You can hear the small noises of every day and you can hear the voice of the flame within for you are one with the flame, one with the light… one with the voice…

You who consume the world are its light. You are its dawn. You are the flame that illuminates… the brightness and the shadows are yours and they dance to the rhythm of that inner voice, that quiet, joyful song within the flame…

And you see that there are other flames, each illuminating the world around them, casting their own light that flickers, blazes, more numerous than the stars.

Yet the light is the same… And you begin to see a pattern that echoes the harmony within.

And yet… There is more…

Far away… tiny on the world's horizon, there is another point of flame. As *you* have become the dawn of flame, another dawn arises, far away… cresting the horizon in a white gold haze…

You watch as it grows from a simple point of fire, to a vast white flame that dwarfs your little light. Rainbows dance across its surface, jewelled colours, harmony of song. A dazzling beauty…

You feel as small as a child reaching out to the beauty you see… yearning towards it as it feeds upon all the flames of the world, consuming them, one by one…

You watch and as the flames are consumed… they are not obliterated but remain, becoming ever brighter, more beautiful, their dance a song of delight and wonder…

Still the white flame grows… purest fire… diamond-clear and brilliant…

You reach out with love… a child of flame….

Reaching out to the brightness and the white-gold flame reaches out to you…

And you too are consumed… subsumed…. Made one with the white fire…

Here there is nothing... and everything... sound and music, joy and beauty... silence and peace ... And love...

There is everything... too much to hold... too much to see and know... and yet you Know it. You taste it.... touch it... feel it... and become it...

As the first flame burned your body in gentleness, this sears your soul... a soul of fire... catching your colours, and the song of your flame in a harmony of light and sound and for a moment you catch a glimpse of the world from within the flame and know its patterns, know its course. You can see the deeper shadows cast by this brightest of lights... deep and stark. And you understand part and purpose, defining the light so that it may be known.

The white flame withdraws, moving high and far. Or perhaps you withdraw, or are sent back into the world. Yet the white gold flame remains with you, part of your fire and your shadows are sharper... deeper. Your own light changed... brighter.. richer....

Your own flame contracts becoming smaller, and smaller, becoming a tiny point of light that you can hold in your hand. In the world around you the shadows deepen once more and the silence returns... yet you can hear a faint echo of that voice of flame... and in your hand you hold a point of light like a jewel that whispers...

You look at the jewel… the only thing you can see in the blackness…. And hear only the whispered song….

You press the jewel to your breast and it sinks into your heart… leaving you in silence and darkness once more and yet within you carry an echo of the One Song… and a Seed of the One Light.

Carry that thought with you…

When you are ready, open your eyes. Move your limbs, look around the room.

The meditation is over.

THE SONG OF THE SOUL

Compose yourself and relax, breathing deeply...

It is the middle of the night and you should really be asleep. You are snuggled under heavy blankets in the dark, warm and cosy. You feel the pressure of the blankets on your body... heavier than a duvet... more comforting... more secure.

There is a faint, exciting smell in the air... a mixture of smells... smoke from the fire, fresh pine branches, the warm smell of spices and food.

Maybe you can smell something cooking... the smell of roasting? Or the warm smell of cakes... or the mince pies?

You are supposed to be asleep but you are as excited as a child...

You hear a faint tinkling sound... like far off bells... you smile to yourself... you do not really believe in Santa Claus anymore, do you? You are too big now...you laugh at yourself gently.

Even so...

The chimes continue... a little louder...but still very faint. You cannot resist opening your eyes...

The room is filled with a soft, pinkish glow... not enough to light the room...but you can see the shapes of the things you know... it is *your* room after all, you know what is here

You can feel the house around you, feel everyone else asleep somehow. The hushed quiet of the world, but the soft light and the silent, sleeping world reminds you of snow.

You throw back the blankets and quietly get out of bed, shivering a little in the cold. Your bones feel the cold these days, you reach for a dressing gown, but it is not where you left it...

Even in the faint glow the room is clearly not your own... and yet it is familiar... very familiar...

Memory stirs... the shapes around you in the soft light are those you recognise from another time... another place... something tugs at the edges of memory...

The silence is punctuated by the clear chimes, very faint. Not sleigh bells... no...

go to the window and part the curtains, looking out into the night. The window sill seems higher than it should... you stand on tiptoes to see...

It has snowed...

A thick, silent blanket shrouds the world, making it unfamiliar. Shapes are hidden by the fallen snow, drifts change the landscape... starlight reflects and sparkles like jewels scattered on the frozen world...

The chimes sound again... delicate... haunting...

Something moves in the street below... something white against the snow... so white that you can see nothing but a stream of warm breath and a pair of great, dark eyes. Gazing straight at you... waiting for you.

You open the window and look down. The cold of the frosty night bites your skin... not unpleasantly... it is fresh and pure, very beautiful.

From the window a staircase of snow descends, step after step, into the street. Into the magical landscape below.

You climb up onto the window ledge, finding it surprisingly easy, and swing your legs over. Your feet look much smaller than usual. Part of your mind wonders what you are doing... you dismiss it... the part of you that remembers how to believe in magic knows exactly what you are doing.

The cold of the snow on your bare feet distracts you and for a moment you wonder if you are dreaming... you must be dreaming...

You shrug and begin to walk down the stairway

made of snow... step after step...

As you do so the ground seems to get bigger... wider... taller.... Or else you are getting smaller with every step...

You look at your hands, and at your bare feet, leaving footprints in the snow. They are a child's hands... child's feet... with each step you are leaving your adult self behind and you are becoming a child once more. Your mind retains all its knowledge and memory... yet it sees now through wonder and enchantment...

As you reach the bottom step you remember the nightclothes you are wearing... the strange shapes of the street are almost familiar in memory beneath their blanket of snow.

But you have no time to think, for there, before you at last, stands the creature white as the snow.

She is not real... she cannot be real... and yet, for you... in this moment... she is.

You can see the warm breath, two plumes of steam and liquid eyes of deepest amber. Her mane is long and flows like water in the breeze... her hooves are silvery white... and the slender horn that crests her forehead is clear as glass.

She holds your eyes.

You want to reach out a hand to touch this

creature... the most beautiful thing you have ever seen. But you dare not... you hardly dare breathe... you are afraid of breaking the moment...

The delicate creature paws the ground and sinks to her knees, she turns her head as if to invite you to mount. You fear she would not bear your weight... then you remember that your body is now that of a child, very small... and you obey the silent summons, sitting astride the waiting creature as the soft chimes again ring out.

As she begins to stand you clutch instinctively at her mane, holding tightly to steady yourself as she rises to her feet. You can feel the heat radiating from her body, keeping you warm. You feel her muscles move beneath you and the hard sharpness of her backbone as she begins to walk her hooves making no sound in the silence of the night.

The snow has started again. Big, heavy snowflakes fall on your skin, feather soft, the gentlest of caresses... lingering a moment then vanishing as they melt. You laugh out loud in sheer delight... you cannot see where you are going, yet you have no fear as the gentle creature carries you into the starlit night.

The chimes sing again... a little louder...

The breeze causes eddies in the snow, parting the falling flakes like a veil... through them you glimpse scenes of childhood days... a snowman.... a sledge.... a pile of snowballs... all, it seems, waiting for you to come and play...

You had forgotten ... yet your body remembers. You can feel in memory the biting cold in your fingers... hear the laughter of children...your laughter.

You can feel the rush of cold on your face as the sledge races down the hill... and the sharp sting of a snowball landing on your skin...

The small pain, the discomfort, did not matter then ... it was worth it. You remember, but recall only joy. You were there...

The scenes open in the snow and are gone... lost in the falling blanket...

The chimes sing again...clear in the night...

The streets have vanished... you ride through trees, the black outlines of their branches stark against the white. You cannot see far, the snow and the darkness close around you, and you move in a small clear space lit, it seems, only by the presence within it. Your presence.

Deeper and deeper you go into the trees...

You feel no cold, the warmth of the creature beneath you flows through your body like a spring morning.

The snow around you sparkles, fleeting diamonds falling like stardust... you laugh aloud again... wondering how long it is since you felt so free to laugh for no other reason but joy...

The chimes are louder now and seem to answer your laughter.

You wonder where you are going... asking the night, speaking aloud without thought...

"You go to seek your song, " says a voice. You do not know whether you have heard it with mind or ears. The voice reminds you of the chimes... and all the voices that you have loved...

On and on you walk together through the night, your body in tune with the creature beneath you, you breath matching the rhythm of her breath, and the trees close about you, weaving their branches, fingers interlaced to hold you safe....

You relax deeper into the moment, almost dreamlike but more real than waking.

Through the branches of the trees a faint glow appears... and the chimes sing louder... a delicate tinkling sound, clear and light.

The trees come closer, forming an arched tunnel, barely wide enough for you to pass...

Snow drifts deep beneath the delicate hooves that

tread so lightly they make barely an imprint in the soft surface.

The tunnel widens and you find yourself in a clearing, a perfect circle of trees. High above the moon shines, clear of the snow clouds and you see that in the centre of the space there is a mound.

The chimes grow ever louder... filling the night air.

The creature treads delicately across the clearing. The moonlight shows you that you are crossing the surface of a frozen pool. The glassy plane is a mirror, and you see reflected within it yourself and your mount with the moonlight above you...a magical image.

You see yourself a child again... there are no lines on your face, no tension in your shoulders... you are young and free and utterly at peace. And yet, a strange excitement is building within you, responding to the music of the chimes.

As you reach the mound in the centre, your companion stops. The mound too is reflected in the icy pool and the steep path that winds around it to its summit also winds down, it seems, into the depths of the earth.

You slide from her back and stand beside her, your hand still buried in the warm, silky mane.

"Now you must choose the way," says the voice.

"Within or without."

You hesitate a moment. The chiming is coming from the centre of the mound... which way should you go? Should you take the path down into the earth? Or up towards the sky?

Which way...?

"Follow your heart," says the voice.

You make your decision and set off along the path...your companion beside you, moving with you.

As the pathway winds around the snowy mound the song of the chimes grows louder and louder...many notes... too many to count... all unique and all equally beautiful together they make a song worthy of heaven.

The path ends with a small space around a great tree... its branches reaching to earth like a weeping willow.

You look up and see the moonlight playing through a million icicles... large and small... swaying together in the breeze. It is from these that the chimes are sounding, tinkling, ringing, tolling like gentle bells. The air is full of a music that wraps itself around your very soul.

You stand, barefoot in the snow in your nightclothes, gazing upon this scintillating orchestra.

"Now comes the third choice," says the voice.

"The third?" you ask.

"The first was when you chose to leave your life behind and follow the song of your soul." Your companion bows her head, the slender, crystal horn catching the moonlight. "Each soul has a song, and every song has a key note. Here you must find the one that is yours. No matter where life leads you, no matter if you are young or old, the timeless note sounds only in the eternal now of your innermost being. Find your song."

You look up and up in wonder, walking round the tree, trying to distinguish the notes from the music. Here and there one of the icicles sings to you and you know you are close... almost... almost...

You lift your hand to touch them... one after the other... and each time the song changes a little... you feel you can almost hear voices within its tones... *almost* understand the song... but not quite.

You move through the hanging branches with delight... each forgotten as you leave it for the next... forgotten like the yesterday of a child, eager as its tomorrow... but present as only a child can be with each note of the song.

For the third time you laugh aloud for sheer joy at the beauty...

And then you hear it...

A note... a single clear chime.

It resonates with everything you are in this moment, answering your joy and laughter....your note... the keynote of your soul's song.

You close your eyes and simply feel it, seeking it with all you are in this moment... all you are in all moments... and then you know....

You turn and face your companion and the deep amber eyes seem to smile.

"Yes," says the voice.

"I had it all along. I brought it here with me... or it brought me here."

The amber eyes glow as they hold your gaze. You reach up to touch the horn of your unicorn as she leans down towards you.

"The path didn't matter. Did it?" asks the wise-child.

"Only the journey matters." She lays her head on your shoulder, and you embrace her beauty, closing your eyes and burying your face in her mane.

When you open your eyes again you hold only your pillow... you are back in your bed.

The dawn glints on an icicle hanging from the roof outside your open window.

You settle back and relax, smiling.... It has been snowing....

When you are ready, feel the room around you, open your eyes and come back into the room.

THE GREY CHAPEL

Breathe deeply, still your thoughts and prepare for a guided journey...

You are standing on a green lawn, surrounded by a grove of trees that mask the surrounding countryside... gnarled oaks, yew and rowan you recognise, other trees you do not.

There is a quality to the light and the clouds that make you feel that you are high upon a mountain, perhaps or a hilltop, but the veil of green prevents you from seeing where you are.

The grass feels pleasantly warm to your bare feet and, looking down, you see that you are dressed in a plain, white robe.

The air is hushed; no sound except the breeze in the trees, an almost subliminal whispering, and the twitter of birds sheltering unseen in their branches.

Before you is a monumental building of silver grey stone. It appears to be circular in form with a square porch full of deep blue shadows.

Similar porches can be glimpsed at either side, marking the quarters, but as you walk around the perimeter of the structure you see that there is only one entrance; the three other squares seem to be windowless chapels and, in fact, you see no windows at all.

A domed roof covers the building, made of precisely shaped blocks of stone, yet light must enter somehow, for it streams through the shadows within, painting a white path on the ground at your feet.

There seems nowhere else to go, no pathway through the dense trees, nothing except this path of light to follow. Taking a deep breath you place your feet upon it and walk towards the porch.

The walls are perfectly smooth...undecorated and stark. Uncompromising. The silence, however, is light and gentle and the feel of the place is one of both peace and power.

Deepest blue shadows cluster around you as you walk between the walls of silver stone and as you enter the porch the silence becomes complete, broken only by the sounds of your life... your heart, your breath, the soft fall of your bare feet and the whisper of the soft fabric of your robe. The light has faded, taking on the quality of starlight.

As you reach the end of the porch you see a curved corridor falling away to left and right, following the contour of the building, with shallow steps leading down either side like the rays of the sun. In front of you a curved inner wall of pure white marble, seamless and polished to an almost mirror-like sheen that reflects you in the dancing shadows.

There is nothing to tell you which way to go, so you call upon all of your knowledge and understanding, and choose to walk deosil, in the direction of the sun. Taking the path that leads to the left you descend the shallow steps to reach the main curve of the corridor.

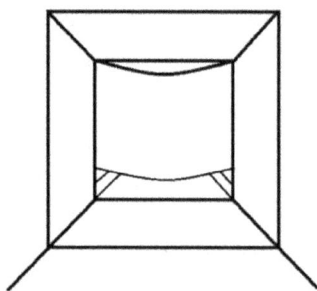

The shadows are deeper here, the silence too. The outer world seems a distant memory. Yet there is no fear... and soon the steps rise before you once more and you find yourself on a landing similar to the first, save that here there is no exit to the left, only a small room.

You enter the room... one of the chapels you saw outside. It is square with a domed roof of its own. In the centre of the ceiling a circular void lets in a shaft of light that falls like a pillar to the ground, seeming too solid and tangible to be the light you know.

It is too bright to see the sky above, yet you feel that a night has passed and a new day begun. Beyond the light you can see a figure against the far wall, white, shadowed blue against the silver stone. A statue perhaps.

You peer through the light and see that is a Child. You cannot see it clearly... the light is too bright and for some reason you fear to enter into it. Yet there is something about that Child that warms your heart, awakening a yearning within you to reach out and touch it, know it...

You rest in contemplation, trying to understand what it is that you see...

After a while you turn and as you reach the place between the steps you see that there is a barred gate in the curved inner wall before you. It seems to be made of some silver metal, closely wrought. You can barely see through the gaps... just enough to glimpse a white light within a central circle.

There is no handle and the gate yields not to your touch.

You step away and continue the clockwise circumambulation, down another set of steps, along another shadowed stretch and up another rise of stairs to a third landing.

You look, but here there is no gate in the curvature

of the inner wall. There is, however, another chapel and you enter inside.

Again the shaft of light bars your way, but this time there is something in the white light, some indefinable quality of a noon in high summer. Beyond the shaft another figure, marble white... you cannot see clearly... a warrior or a hunter, perhaps... you do not know what it is but there is something of courage and endurance about the stance... something you recognise.

Instinctively you straighten your spine, drawing yourself up to match that example... somehow it reminds you of yourself, the stronger side that the world seldom seems.

Again you stand in contemplation of what this might mean, before turning back and continuing along the path, down another set of stairs, through the shadows and once more up to the fourth landing. You have begun to get a feel for the place and its shape speaks to you. You are lost in thought as you walk into the chapel. The shaft of light, pure white, yet has the feeling of sunset.

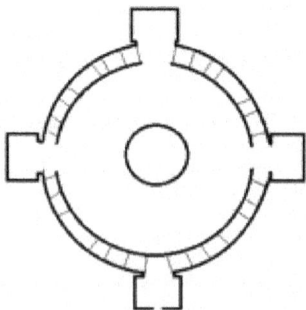

You sense, rather than see, the colour of blood on an unseen horizon and the figure on the wall speaks of death.

Yet the building does not end here... it is a circle, without beginnings, whose path leads up and down, through shadow to light in an endless round.

The figure seems to have suffered. Is death a welcome release perhaps, or simply another step in the dance? You consider these things without fear, feeling them in your own life echoing into the future.

Turning, you face the corridor and see another gate. This one stands open, yet the way is barred.

The figure is dressed in a simple white robe, identical to your own. His hands are folded on his breast and hidden in his sleeves, his head shaven, his eyes look into your own.

You feel naked before his gaze. There are no adornments, nothing to show his office, yet he exudes power. You feel you should kneel before such might, yet the memory of the warrior comes to you and you stand straight, holding yourself tall before him. His eyes are kind, radiating love and a gentle severity. You suddenly know the meaning of awe.

No words are spoken, yet his voice sounds in your being. You may not pass this way. Your time has not yet come.

Beyond him you see the central circle, molten gold

illuminated by the brilliance of the light that streams in from above.

This is the place of the Cosmic Christ... the Christ as Magus, here at the navel of the worlds.

He raises his hands and within them he holds a Cup. Light seems to stream into it. You think of the stories of the Grail Chapel and wonder... you think of the entrance to this place that somehow itself seems to echo the shape of the Cup. So, perhaps, does the shape of this Temple...and yet, there is more...

Threads of understanding begin to come together in your mind and heart as the Priest holds the Cup towards you with a smile.

Whom does the Grail serve?

You do not know if the thought is his or yours...or if there is a difference...

You bend your head, covering his hands with yours, and, closing your eyes against its brilliance, you drink the liquid Light.

When you open your eyes once more, both Priest and gate are gone. Only the smooth curve of white marble before you and the silver path of light at your feet.

Turning, you find yourself back at the entrance and, taking a last look around, you follow the path back through the blue shadows of the porch... back into the glade where now the sun has set and the moon rides high and silver in the heavens, casting its pathway on the dew-damp grass.

You feel the cool wetness on your feet, and look up at the wheel of stars, closing your eyes and drinking in the silver light of life.

Slowly you become aware once more of your body, feel the earth beneath your feet... and when you are ready, come back into the room, carrying with you the essence of your journey...

HAWK OF THE MORNING

Compose yourself and relax, breathing deeply...

You stand on the green earth, tall as a tree, head reaching to the heavens. Bathed in golden sunlight, caressed by a gentle rain. Your hands form the sign of the dove before your breast, wrists crossed, palms facing inwards, thumbs crossed and interlocked.

Over your heart centre, at the solar plexus, is a flower... a rose... not a garden rose, but wild... a single crown of petals of the purest pink, touched with gold... the colours of sunset. At its heart it is a deep, rich gold.

Watch the rose as its petals deepen in colour, and one by one fall, caught by a breeze and carried away lightly.

The centre fades and falls, a golden mist, to the ground, leaving behind an ovoid sphere of velvet darkness...like a rose hip... pulsing to the same cadence as your heartbeat, full of possibility for growth.

Now, send your vision down through the stem of the rose... down through your body to the green earth.

The stems twine around you, spiralling down and through your frame, and your thought is silver as it follows their path.

Follow the stem down to the roots of the rose, firmly planted in the warm ground. Feel how you are rooted here, how you are nourished by the earth, part of the earth...

Let your thoughts follow the roots into that warm darkness, becoming the roots, spreading through the ground...feeling all the glorious diversity, the life of plant and rock, the creatures that live upon the earth and under the earth. Feel the moisture seeping through the soil and stones, the blood of earth.

Feel the shared cycle of life as a buzzing, vibrant energy... a dance of life, death and rebirth... and know yourself to be part of this diverse unity.

Sink deeper into the heart of earth and see there the red heat of fire, flames like the petals of a rose of deepest red, contained physical energy, pressurised within the sphere of earth seeking to find a way to the surface.

The flames leap at your touch.

Now draw that fire up through your roots, like blood through the veins, carrying motes of inner fire like rubies... up through the earth, through your feet, your calves, through your thighs... let it settle at the base of the spine around the genitals. See it as a rosebud... watch as the bud grows and swells, bursting into life... Clear and red, bright as blood...alive as flame... the petals unfold into a perfect red rose. Watch it open there, rooted in the well of earth.

Feel the energy of Creation within you and Know you are part of that magnificent Life.

Draw that reddest of roses up the spine to the heart and let it rest there, filling the dark velvet space with its vibrant energy and life.

Now, send your inner vision up the stems of the rose, seeing it silver, flowing through the spiralling branches that twine themselves around and through your body. Pass through the chest, the throat... pass through the eyes and through the brain and emerge through the top of the skull to the crown.

You are crowned with a circlet of rose-stems, nine thorns rest upon your head... the thorns of the Ego.

Feel the golden sun warming you, nourishing the inner life, symbol of the Source of all. Taste the air around, fresh and clean... air that holds you and carries the breath of life to your lungs and sends it coursing through your veins.

The touch of raindrops, gentle on your skin,

connecting heaven and earth through you... water of life.

The Light streams down and a flower forms ... crowning you with the purity of the white rose...you watch the petals unfold, one by one, revealing a centre of purest gold... a chalice that catches the raindrops... catches and reflects the sunlight within its pristine whiteness.

Now, draw this flower down to the heart... feel its descent through the head, touching the mind, vision and voice with its clarity as you draw it downwards.

Let it rest at the heart centre with the red rose, banishing the last of the velvet darkness...and watch as they become one. The red and the white softly melding, flowing together... each colour calling to the essence of the other, blending together to become a single, resplendent rose of the purest pink, touched with gold; the colours of dawn. At its heart it glows with golden light.

Let it rest there a moment, filling your body with its light and beauty, the melded energies of earth and heaven suffusing your being, bathing your body, your senses and your mind in a luminous and vibrant clarity.

Feel all the energy of the heavens and the earth flooding your body, your mind and your heart with bright beauty and the depth of the life of which you are a part.

Feel this life rushing through you like a clean wind,

or a stream, cleansing, carrying with it untold energy that fills you with Life until you feel you can hold no more,

Watch as the dove formed by your hands carry the rose upwards, through the chest, through the voice, through vision... golden in its flight. Let it lift the rose through the mind to the crown... seeing the dawn glowing in its petals... and let it rest there a moment... then offer your Rose to the Light.

As you watch the nine thorns become translucent and fade away, leaving only the resplendent beauty of the Rose.

Watch as the dove becomes the Hawk of the Morning, strong, free... golden...carrying the rose... your Rose... up, and up, spiralling into the Sun. As you lose sight of the Hawk in the brilliance, the rain turns to gold and you are bathed in the Beauty of the Light.

Slowly you become aware once more of your body, feel the earth beneath your feet... and when you are ready, come back into the room, carrying with you the essence of your journey...

THE MANY PETALLED CROWN

Close your eyes, relax and prepare for an inner journey, breathing deeply and easily.

You stand on a green mound by a sunlit sea. Far below you is a pristine shore of white sand, you hear the echoes as the waves wash gently, rhythmically, against the base of the cliff. The soft, rushing sound of water in the shingle whispers in the clear air of morning.

The sky is a pure blue, the colour of the Lady's robe. Forget-me-not blue, and at its heart, as in the flower, the golden circle of the sun.

The cry of a distant gull touches your heart with an unfathomable yearning, yet you are here, now, in this time and in this place. There is no other thought in your mind, only here, only this moment.

You close your eyes and with sight absent, other senses seem to come to the fore. The salt tang of the air touches your lips and tongue, warm rays caress your face, the soft thrumming of the waves seems to reach through the very earth beneath your feet, finding its way within and dancing with your breath.

The air smells fresh and clean, like the first morning of the world. You stand, simply drinking in the moment, the world around you, feeling yourself at its heart, feeling it within your body.

In the distance you can hear music playing, the delicate tones of a harp, beautiful in its simplicity, as if played by a gifted child, a wise child, one who sees clearly beyond the veils of Light. The purity of the simple song draws you. You listen... silent... barely daring to move.

You are afraid to move and break the spell, yet almost against your will you are drawn to the music. Like a sleepwalker you move towards the edge of the cliff.

There is a path, narrow and steep, tufts of sea thrift grow beside it, nodding their bright pink heads in the breeze. You begin to descend.

The way is steep. Small stones roll at your feet, bouncing down the cliff face as you walk. Tiny fragments of rock dislodged with every step. Your shoes, black and shiny, are covered in the white dust of chalk.

You stop and sit on the flower covered bank. The perfume of crushed thyme fills the air and you notice the tiny, lilac flowers all around you. Removing your shoes, leaving them there, you stretch your bare feet, wiggling your toes… You feel like a child. You do not need them.

You lie back against the fragrant green and rest for a while, perfectly happy, as the sun warms your skin.

Still the music haunts you. It is very soft, so soft you had almost forgotten it was there, calling you onwards. You rise and continue down the steep path. Looking up you can see the towering white cliffs, sparkling in the clear light. You think of the shores of Albion and wonder if that is where you are… or only where you think you might be? It does not matter. You are here. It is all you need to know.

Beside a turn in the path stream bubbles crystal clear from the rock face, gathering in a small pool. In the bottom of the pool you can see many offerings, small gifts, coins, tablets etched with words. Beside the stream is an ancient cup. You fill it from the stream and drink from it.

The water is cold and sweet, you can feel on your tongue, in your throat, rich and fragrant, a nourishing draught, quite unlike any water you have tasted before. It is a draught of liquid Light. You feel it flowing through you, feel lit up from the inside, as if you shine softly like a star.

You replace the cup. You feel you should leave a gift and feel in your pockets, not knowing what is there. It must be something that holds meaning to you, something of value, not in payment, but in gratitude for what you have received.

Your fingers find an object, feeling its lines and edges. You draw it from your pocket and look at it as it rests in your hands. You had forgotten it was there... yet it has always been there. You always carry it. You smile, knowing what it represents; knowing what it means to you... then cast it in the pool. The ripples spread out across the surface, obscuring the bottom. Small streams of light wash over the edges of the pool, spilling onto the grassy bank and where they touch flowers spring up.

You continue down the path, following it to the beach following the song that seems to hold an echo of the music of the spring. The dry sand is white and soft underfoot, sun warmed and pleasant. A little way ahead the cliff reaches out towards the sea and you see the dark mouth of a small cave. You walk towards it, leaving footprints in the sand, following the song.

Outside the cave there seem to be large boulders, yet as you draw closer you see that they are piles of clothes. Whole suits and dresses, smocks and ball gowns, judges robes, uniforms... every imaginable type of clothing that bears the mark of position or office... like heaped skins divested by their owners.

The music takes on an insistent note and you feel

you understand. Stripping off your clothes you add them to the pile, feeling as if you have erased a deeper layer of your identity you stand naked in the sunlight. Once more you hear the cry of the gulls and look up.

From above a crown of petals, purest white, is falling towards you, from the wings of the birds. It settles about your brow, crowing you with beauty.

You walk forward towards the cave. A sheet of water veils the entrance, so clear it is almost invisible except for the captured fire of the sunlight. You stand in the shallow stream that cuts a channel like a pathway, your feet sinking slightly in the wet sand, as if you are part of the earth, the earth takes you into itself.

The music calls you onward and you walk, crowned and naked through the sparkling veil. As you do so, the water clothes you in a robe of the finest and rainbow silk, the shifting hues almost impossible to follow with the eye.

The floor of the cave is strewn with polished stones, cool and smooth. You feel light and free in the robes, unconstricted.

You move easily, noticing for the first time that with your clothing you seem to have left behind the stresses and strains of daily life, with your shoes you left the aches and pains, when you left the cliff top you left the cares and worries behind... you realise that with every step the descent into this cavern has been one of giving up the things you are so used to that you did not even know they were there.

You follow the music still, deeper into the darkness of the cavern, sure footed even in the shadows. You are at home here, in the heart of the earth.

Gradually a light fills the space, a shaft of Light that reaches through the whole height of the cliff... a straight path to the sky. Is from this that the music emanates.

Above the shaft the golden orb of the sun sits high in the heavens, a single ray directed and held within the narrow shaft, focussed so bright you can barely see,

Drawn still by the whispering song you step into the Light. All fear seems to dissolve, all pain dissipate... the weight of worlds seems to lift from you and you are as a babe again, bathed in the purity of golden Light.

Stay... stay as long as you wish... feel the shadows gilded and the hurts healed.... And know that this Light fills you always.

So mote it be.

When you are ready, come back, open your eyes, breathe deeply... feel yourself back in the room renewed.

A CALL TO ACTION

Over a number of years, at every workshop held within the Living Land, we have invited our Companions to join us in a guided journey that is close to our hearts.

We invite you to join with us now for a few moments, opening that portal in the heart and mind through which all may pass, that together we may weave a Web of Light.

At this time, when our word is in turmoil, when we are challenged by fear and at a time of pandemic, when the bounty of our planet is being stretched beyond endurance and so many of its creatures face extinction, let us add our voices to the Web that is being woven by Seekers of Light of many paths and traditions, all around the earth.

Alone, we can do little, but when hearts come together to work in harmony, we can change the world, even if it is only by changing ourselves.

Wherever the sacredness of the earth is

remembered, wherever the ancient places are revered, wherever a single heart turns away from fear and hatred to Love, a point of Light is added to the Web. Let this moment become a shining point in the Web of Light.

***

If you can, please light a candle and use its flame as a focus. If possible, place three small stones around it in a triangle. Imagine that these stones are seeds that can grow and flower and see them as symbols of your intent.

Read the meditation slowly, leaving plenty of time for the imagination to take flight. Whatever you can imagine is real within the mind and can be brought through into a more concrete reality.

Now, find a place of peace within your hearts... and prepare for meditation. Let us weave the Web of Light together.

THE WEB OF LIGHT

Feel your body, rooted in earth. Feel the air as you breathe, in... and out... filling your body with its gift. Your body is a creature of earth. Your soul is not of the earth. It is of a finer substance, your life no more than a chapter in its story. It is eternal... your body a temporary garment that it wears. Let it fly free...

In your mind's eye, see yourself within a Temple amongst friends. Now see the 'soul' of the Temple. It too is other than its body. Its pillars are a grove of standing stones in a vast space filled with Light. Its shape mirrors the universe...

A circle at your feet maps the evolution of the soul... and above the central point there is a single, brilliant flame that reaches up into the night.

Let your mind follow the path lit by the flame and rise, higher and higher... passing through the roof and out into the darkness of space.

Around you, the stars wheel in the heavens, bright points of dancing light against the indigo sky. The land spreads out beneath you, a living shadow that reaches as far as you can see and beyond...

From the central light, silver flame spreads, pulsing, across the earth in a great web of light. Where the threads cross, you know that stones have been set, groves, mounds and pools... places of worship... sacred centres of all paths, faiths and denominations, harmonising the flow of cosmic Life and Light.

You are part of that Web, part of its warp and weft. You are a tender of the Flame.

Feel the life of the earth coursing through its strands... and through you. Give yourself to its glory. See the web blaze bright and clean... burning away all shadows, healing all rifts and lighting the land.

Within you, the flame also burns...

Its essence is a steady point of brilliance in your heart, small as a seed, but vast as the universe. You are its guardian.

Now slowly, gently, return your mind to the Inner Temple, carrying the vision of Light within.

If you so choose, you may continue with the meditation by becoming a voice for the voiceless...

SILENT VOICES

As an addition to the Web of Light meditation, we asked our Companions to give voice to some of the silent voices of the earth... would you speak for them too?

Take a moment to think of the earth and its creatures. For the life of the planet that manifests in a myriad ways. For the flowers and trees, for the animals, for the people who suffer. For that which can only speak to a listening heart. For the voiceless.

"I speak for the lonely. Those that think they are separate from the One. I speak for the light to shine upon their hearts and open them to love. I speak for their voices to be heard, and their prayers to lead them onto the lighted path. I speak for the bereft and alone to lift their hearts to love. I ask that they be guided on the path to find the wondrous gate to all that is true. I speak for love, all that is and will ever be." *Jordis Fasheh.*

"I will speak for those who seek the Light. I join with you as a seeker of light and of truth, in this, the winter of my years. I see the beauty in all that we are and all that we can become. I reach out to join you in this beautiful dance of life itself with the One. As we continue our incredible journey together, we understand that we are not outside the One, but the One seeing with many eyes and many hearts, and joined in a higher purpose-the alchemy of a life lived fully in concert with all that exists within this universe." *Anne Copeland.*

Will you add your voice? If so, choose for whom you will speak. Speak for the lost or the lonely, the war-torn lands, the children who weep...for the trees felled for profit and the oceans despoiled... give voice to whoever and whatever cannot speak out for themselves. Then, in your own words, speak for them now.

Please stand and let your voice be heard, resonating through the Web, a song in the silence, an affirmation of hope in the darkest night.

When you have spoken, sit quietly for a few moments, only then *extinguish your candle to end the meditation.*

Take the three small stones and keep them with you until you find a place where it feels right to leave one. There, 'plant' your 'seed' of intent, as a symbol of hope and healing.

We thank you for joining with us at this time.

"We offer ourselves as vessels, in service to the One. We see Its Perfection in the unfolding of Divine Will in accordance with the Laws of Being. Our lives flow from the Source; we stand in the presence of the All-Knowing, looking beyond the Veil in faith and trust. Through knowledge and experience, we seek Wisdom. From illusion we turn towards Truth. We journey from love to Love. We add our Light to the Web, renewing our dedication to the Light." *The Silent Eye.*

MAY THE LIGHT SHINE ALWAYS
UPON AND WITHIN YOU.

ABOUT THE AUTHOR

Sue Vincent is a Yorkshire born writer, who has been immersed in the Mysteries all her life. She is a teacher and Director of The Silent Eye, a modern Mystery School. Sue co-authored The Mystical Hexagram with Dr G. M. Vasey and many other books, both alone and with her co-Director, Stuart France.

The writing partnership of France and Vincent has a peculiar alchemy of humour, scholarship and vision that has given birth to many books, including the Triad of Albion, Doomsday and Lands of Exile series'.

Sue has a lasting love-affair with the landscape of Albion, the hidden country of the heart. She lives in Buckinghamshire, having been stranded there some years ago due to an accident with a blindfold, a pin and a map. She is currently owned by a small dog who also blogs.

You can follow their adventures online at scvincent.com or franceandvincent.com and find Sue on Twitter @SCVincent.

If you have enjoyed this book, please consider leaving a review on Amazon or Goodreads.

THE SILENT EYE

The Silent Eye School of Consciousness is a modern Mystery School, founded by Steve Tanham, that celebrates the inherent magic in living and being.

With students around the world, the School offers a fully supervised and practical correspondence course that explores the self through guided inner journeys and daily exercises.

The Silent Eye also offers regular workshops that combine ritual, talks and informal gatherings within the landscape, bringing the teachings to life in a vivid and exciting format.

The Silent Eye operates on a not-for-profit basis.

Full details of the School, the distance learning course and upcoming events may be found on the official website: thesilenteye.co.uk.

❖

Don and Wen thought it was just a day out in an ancient landscape wrought in earth and stone, walking the sacred ways of the Old Ones. They could not know what mysteries would unfold as the birds led them deep into the legendary history of Albion.

As the veils thin and waver, time shifts and the present is peopled with shadowy figures from the past, weaving their tales through a quest for understanding and opening wide the doors of perception for those who seek to see beyond the surface of reality…

Doomsday
The Ætheling Thing   Dark Sage   Scions of Albion

What exactly were the Norse gods doing on a supposedly Christian artefact that looked more like a standing stone than a cross?

Don is drawn to investigate, questioning the history of the Blessed Isles of Albion, while Wen determines to restore the position of one particular stone.

Which would have been alright if Ben hadn't gone back for the gun…

❖

Lands of Exile
But 'n' Ben   Beck 'n' Call   Kith 'n' Kin

While Ben, fast becoming a folk hero, languishes in Bakewell Gaol, Don and Wen are on holiday… or 'on the run' if Bark Jaw-Dark and PC 963 Kraas, hot in pursuit, are to be believed.

From England to Scotland and Ireland, the officers of the Law follow the trail of the erratic couple.

But who is the shadowy figure, hovering beyond sight?

What is his interest in a small standing stone and just how many high-level strings can he pull… and why?

BOOKS BY FRANCE AND VINCENT

Triad of Albion
The Initiate - Heart of Albion - Giants Dance

The Doomsday Series
The Ætheling Thing - Dark Sage - Scions of Albion

Lands of Exile
But 'n' Ben – Beck 'n' Call = Kith 'n' Kin

Graphic Novels
Mister Fox: The Legend
Mister Fox & the Demon Dogs
Mister Fox and the Green Man
Mister Fox: Winter's Tail

Loreweavers
An Imperious Impulse: Coyote Tales

By Stuart France

Poetry/mythology
Crucible of the Sun: The Mabinogion Retold

Spiritual Journey
The Living One: Caravan to Cairns

Philosophy
Slivers of Søren: Testaments to Truth
Pieces of Nietzsche: A Thinker's Bias
Nuances of Nicoll: The Keys to Heaven

By Sue Vincent

Mythology
The Osiriad: Myths of Ancient Egypt

Esoteric Fantasy
Swords of Destiny

Meditation
Petals of the Rose: Guided Journeys

Poetry and humour
Notes from a Small Dog: Four Legs on Two
Laughter Lines: Life from the Tail End
Doggerel: Life with the Small Dog
Pass the Turkey!: Christmas with the Small Dog
Life Lines: Poems from a Reflection

With Dr G. Michael Vasey
The Mystical Hexagram: The Seven Inner Stars of Power

Available via Amazon worldwide

www.ingramcontent.com/pod-product-compliance
Lightning Source LLC
Chambersburg PA
CBHW060532030426
42337CB00021B/4217